CATS

CATS

by Howard Loxton

Illustrated by Gwen Green
and John Green

Willowisp Press

Published in 1986 by Willowisp Press, Inc.
401 E. Wilson Bridge Road, Worthington, Ohio 43085

This Book Fair Edition published by arrangement with
Granada Publishing Limited
London, England

ISBN 0-87406-083-4

Printed and bound in Italy by
New Interlitho, Milan

10 9 8 7 6 5 4 3 2 1

Granada ®
Granada Publishing ®

Contents

Cats as Pets

Cats, and especially kittens, look so beautiful and are so cuddly and friendly that it is difficult to resist wanting one as a pet. However, it is important to think hard before getting one because it will become your responsibility to care for it for many years.

When choosing a cat, the time that can be devoted to it must be taken into account. For example, long-hairs will require more time for grooming. Oriental types will usually demand more of your attention.

A cat's character is not so clearly defined by breed as a dog's. It depends on the cat itself and the way it has been reared.

Kittens should stay with their mothers until eight weeks old.

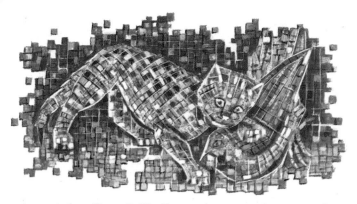

A mosaic from Pompeii. The Romans kept cats to keep rats, mice, and snakes out of their houses and food stores. It was probably the Romans who introduced domestic cats to Britain.

Kittens with runny eyes or noses or signs of diarrhea should be avoided, for this may indicate disease. A bloated tummy may be a sign of worms. A cat scratching excessively probably has fleas. A discharge in the ears may be a symptom of ear mites. It is easy to get rid of a light infestation of these parasites. But it is important to check carefully that the kitten is otherwise clean and well. A sickly-looking cat may only give its owner a large vet's bill and heartbreak.

Kittens should not leave their mother until they are eight weeks old. They will then have been weaned and probably taught by their mother to use a litter tray. Any new kitten (or stray or adult cat) should be taken to the vet as soon as possible for a check up. Be sure that the breeder or vet gives a certificate to show that the kitten has been vaccinated against feline infectious enteritis—it is a dangerous disease.

As a new addition to a family, a kitten will need litter and a litter tray, food, and water bowls. A basket or a cardboard box with an old blanket in it will serve as a cat bed.

Cats always need clean water and about one ounce of food a day for each pound of body weight. A kitten or pregnant cat can have more. An eight-week-old kitten should have four small meals a day because its stomach is only the size of a walnut. By the end of a year it can have all its food in one or two meals a day. Stale food must be removed. Food bowls should be thoroughly washed.

Cats are very clean and always washing themselves, but they need a regular brushing—longhairs must be groomed daily. A cat which goes outdoors should have a collar and a name tag bearing the owner's address.

Regular brushing will cut down on fur balls and fur on furniture. Tangles should be combed out. Stroking the cat with your hand or a piece of velvet will add a final gloss to the shorthaired coats.

The collar should have an elastic section so that the cat can wiggle free if it catches on anything. An indoor cat should have a scratching block or post to exercise its claws. The claws may need to be trimmed occasionally. Cats like to eat grass. It helps them to bring up hair balls formed from hair they swallow in washing.

Things to look out for when grooming a cat are ear discharges, fleas (black specks of flea dirt are more easily seen than the fleas themselves), and any injuries. General weariness, vomiting, lack of appetite, and the partial closing of the membrane in the corner of the eye are all signs of possible illness. A vet will give advice on how to give ear drops to deal with mites, to treat for fleas with powder or aerosol, and to give pills for worms.

A grown cat should never be picked up just by its neck. Its body must always be supported from below. Holding a cat like this will be comfortable for the cat and its the owner.

The Cat as Hunter

Cats have very flexible skeletons which enable them to twist and turn, powerful muscles to jump and leap, strong claws to give a firm grip, and acute sight and hearing. All these things equip them to be very efficient hunters.

The cat is a carnivore, a meat-eater, although even in the wild it will eat some plants. It is adept at catching mice and other small rodents and may also catch birds, flies, snakes, fish, and even large mammals such as rabbits. The chasing and pouncing play of kittens with their mother and siblings is all part of their training for the hunt. Instinct restrains them from actually hurting each other. This instinct will also often operate when cats are playing with people they know well.

It is natural for a cat to hunt mice or birds, and they should never be blamed for doing so. Some cats will even bring their catch home as a present. The cat's victim can have more of a chance to escape if a bell is hung on the cat's collar so that it can be heard coming.

The iris of a cat's eye closes to a slit in bright light (1) and opens wide to let in more light when it is dim (2). The membrane from the corner of the eye cuts out ultra-brightness and may also indicate sickness if it remains permanently raised (3).

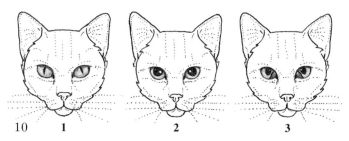

1   2   3

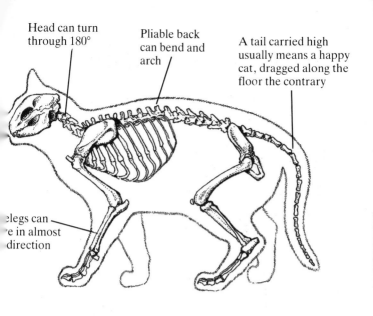

Head can turn
through 180°

Pliable back
can bend and
arch

A tail carried high
usually means a happy
cat, dragged along the
floor the contrary

legs can
e in almost
direction

Cats cannot see colors as clearly as humans. Stationary objects may not be so distinct to them. But they rarely miss a movement and can see in very little light so that they can hunt at night. They can hear over a wider range of sound than humans—to pitches two or three times higher and with greater sensitivity. They can focus their moveable ears upon a sound and locate the exact position of its source.

A development within the ear gives cats a superb sense of balance, demonstrated not only by their acrobatic skills, but by the fact that, unlike many dogs and humans, cats do not get travel sick in cars.

Their highly developed sense of smell helps them to identify things at long distances. A cat will sniff another animal, or its owner returning home. It is finding out from small scent traces where the animal or person has been and whom they have met.

11

The Rise of the Cat

The earliest distinctly cat type so far discovered emerged 40 million years ago, long before true cats appeared. Lynx-sized, it looked like a modern cat, but had much bigger teeth. From it developed the sabre-toothed tiger, which became extinct in pre-historic times. Either from this or an even earlier joint ancestor came all our modern cats including the lion, tiger, leopards, jaguar, cheetah, lynx, puma, bobcat, and all the smaller cats.

There are 36 different species in all, widely different in size, from the 13-foot long (including the tail) Siberian tiger to the 24-inch long rusty spotted cat of the Indian subcontinent. Each has developed to fit a particular environment and way of life, but their individual differences are fewer than their similarities. They are all quite clearly cats.

Puma

Lynx

European Wildcat

African Wildcat

No one is certain which of the smaller cats was the origin of our domestic cat. Mummified African wildcats and jungle cats have been found among the domestic cat mummies of ancient Egypt. The European wildcat looks very much like a big domestic tabby. It just has a larger skull and teeth and a rounded tip to its tail. In Asia one of the small spotted cats may have been another ancestor.

The cat became domesticated much later than the dog or cow. It has been consciously bred only recently. The pet in your home is still little changed from the wild animal.

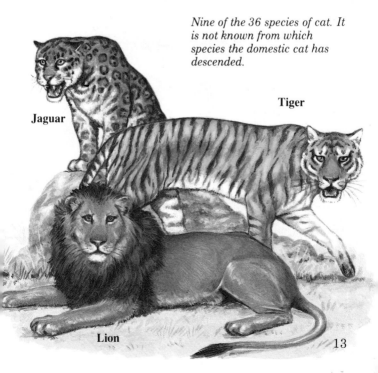

Nine of the 36 species of cat. It is not known from which species the domestic cat has descended.

Jaguar

Tiger

Lion

13

Over 4,000 years ago the cat became the object of a religious cult in Egypt. By about 1800 BC there is clear evidence that it was being kept as a domestic animal. Cats kept away rodents and snakes and were also trained to retrieve wild fowl for hunters. The Egyptians treated cats with great respect and affection. Killing one was considered a serious crime.

When a cat died it was elaborately mourned, mummified and buried with honor. The sun god Ra was sometimes shown in cat form as the victor over the snake, which represented darkness. The goddess Mafdet, protectress of the pharaoh, was also depicted as a cat.

The Egyptians tried to stop their cats being exported, but they reached Rome where they were appreciated as rodent catchers. Cats were also highly regarded by the Saxons and the Welsh. In one

monastic order cats were the only pet that nuns were allowed to keep.

Cats are clean creatures and deposit their waste away from the places where they live. But in our homes they need to be given some training. A cat can be trained to use a litter tray or to go outdoors. The tone of voice will usually let the cat know what the owner is saying. A light tap with a finger is the nearest anyone should get to hitting it. A cat must know the rules from the start. It must never be permitted to do something one day and not another. Cats do not like being confused.

Right: Bast was the most important of the Egyptian cat deities. At the great temple at Bubastis, on the Lower Nile, sacred cats kept in the courtyard were carefully watched for any sign that might indicate a message from the goddess.

The worship of Bast goes back to before 1780 BC and still flourished at the suppression of paganism in the Roman Empire in AD 392.

Thousands upon thousands of embalmed and mummified cats lined the underground catacombs at Bubastis.

Left: A cat will wait patiently for hours until its prey appears.

15

Breeding Cats

Unlike dogs, cats have not been bred for different tasks such as guarding, hunting, or tracking. Exotic or unusual types have attracted attention and been highly valued. But it was not until the last century that people began to deliberately control breeding to produce particular types. Body shape, fur type, and coat color and pattern have now been produced in almost every possible combination. A small number of cats are involved in creating a new breed. Some personality characteristics may be passed on in a breeding line. But as a rule character is largely influenced by the way a kitten is reared and trained.

The first cat shows were held in the 1870s. Since

At a cat show you can usually see many different breeds.

Genes are the parts of a living cell that control what is inherited from generation to generation. Some are said to be dominant. This means that a cat is certain to have the characteristics, such as color, carried by the dominant gene. Some genes are recessive which means that they will only be effective if both genes passed on by the parents are also recessive.

Three examples of how genes are passed on to offspring are shown right. Each parent passes one of a pair of genes on to its young. The gene for tabby marking (D) is dominant over black (d), so DD and Dd are tabbies, and dd is black. In each of the three cases, because the genetic makeup of the parents differs, the number of blacks in a litter changes.

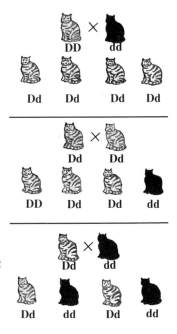

then organizations have become established around the world which lay down the "standards"—the exact descriptions—to which a cat of particular type must conform. They decide whether a new mixture of characteristics should be recognized as a new breed. In the United States there are a number of cat associations which sometimes promote slightly different standards.

A careful record is kept of the parentage of "pure-bred" cats, known as their pedigree. A pure-bred cat will produce kittens true to type if matched with another of its kind. However non-pedigree, or mongrel cats, can make just as attractive pets.

Short-haired Cats

All the wild members of the cat family have short coats. Domestic cats that go wild soon revert to short fur. Shorthair is probably very like western domestic cats of centuries past.

American domestic cats were originally taken out by emigrants from Europe. But there is now a distinctively different American short-haired breed. There is a sleeker group of breeds known as Foreign Shorthairs and there are a few other short-haired breeds outside these groups.

There are many cats kept as household pets which are short-haired. Few non-pedigree cats can match the standards to which show cats must conform, however attractive they may be.

White British Shorthairs may have orange eyes, blue eyes, or one of each (odd-eyed).

Blue British Shorthair

British Shorthairs

This breed has a compact, powerfully-muscled body with a broad chest, short legs, rounded paws, and a shortish tail that is thick at the base and rounded at the tip. The head is round and broad with a short, straight nose, firm chin, and round-tipped ears which are set well apart, and large round eyes, which are orange or copper colored. The neck is short and thick.

The British Blue is a breed which has a reputation for gentleness and intelligence. Although popular

Black British Shorthair

Cream British Shorthair

Blue Cream British Shorthair

among those who enter cat shows it is not very common today. Its coat is often more plush than in other colors—like deep-piled velvet—and its broad head and short nose often meets the standard more closely. The fur is blue-grey of medium to light shade all over, without any trace of stripes, spots, or white hairs. Nose and paws should match the fur in color.

In France a breed known as the Chartreux is very similar. The French allow green eyes and permit the coat to be any shade of blue.

Other self-color coats are the White, Black, and Cream. White British Shorthairs must be pure white with no trace of cream or any other color. Nose and paw pads are pink. This variety may also have blue eyes, or even one eye orange and one eye blue. Unfortunately blue-eyed white cats are often deaf, though kittens with a trace of another color in their coat are not usually affected. The color trace often disappears leaving a pure white cat when adult.

The Black must have fur jet black to the roots,

black nose, and black paw pads. Kittens sometimes have a brownish tinge to the coat which disappears in good pedigree cats as they get older. In adults the brownish color is a definite fault. It is sometimes a result of too much sunbathing. Cream cats should have an even-colored coat that does not become too red. The Blue Cream variety has the two colors softly intermingled in the coat with a blue nose and blue or pink paw pads.

Bi-colored British Shorthairs

Red and White

Blue and White

Black and White

Bi-colored Shorthairs are cats with a two-color coat of white and a darker color in distinctly separate patches. They cannot be more than half white or two-thirds colored. Patching should be across the face. A white streak should run down from the forehead. Black, blue, red, and even cream may be combined with white, but there must be no odd hairs. In the U.S. they are also known as parti-colored.

Tortoiseshell cats have a three-color coat: black clearly patched with cream and red on the face, body, legs, and tail. Nose and paw pads may be pink, black, or patched. A cream or red streak or "blaze" on the face is desirable. Tortoiseshells are nearly always female, and a self-colored Black or Cream will make a suitable mate in breeding. The kittens are born with dark fur which later becomes patchy as it grows. The

**Tortoiseshell
British Shorthair**

**Smoke
British Shorthair**

Tortoiseshell and White has the three-color pattern patched on a white coat. Cheeks, top of the head, ears, back, tail, and parts of the legs are colored. The belly, chest, chin, and part of the legs are white. It too is usually female.

The Smoke Shorthair may have an upper coat of either black or blue with an undercoat of pale silver. When moving the undercoat shows through, but if the cat is still it looks as though it has only dark fur. Both the undercoat and topcoat of the Tipped British Shorthair are white, but every top hair on the back, flanks, head, ears, and tail has a colored tip. These may be any one of the colors already described or brown, chocolate, or lilac. Nose and paw pads should be pink or match the tipping.

Tipped
British Shorthair

Tortoiseshell and White
British Shorthair

Tabby markings are of two kinds: striped like a tiger and blotched like taffeta or watered silk. The striped pattern, like that of the European Wildcat, is now officially known as the mackerel tabby. The blotched, which probably developed from it, is called the standard or classic tabby. The standard tabby pattern must have three stripes running down the back with shapes like a butterfly's wings across the shoulders and a blotch like an oyster on the flank encircled by unbroken rings. Legs and tail are evenly ringed. The face has fine pencil markings on the cheeks, an unbroken line from the corner of the eye, an M-shaped mark on the forehead, and a dark line over the top of the head. The mackerel has similar head markings, only one stripe along the spine and narrow stripes down to the belly.

Tabby Shorthairs can be brown, red, or silver and of either pattern. Brown Tabbies have coppery brown fur with a dense black pattern, a brick red nose, and black or brown paw pads. Red Tabbies have red (orange) fur with deep markings, brick red eyes, and deep red paw pads. Silver Tabbies are silver-coated

Spotted Shorthair

Red Tabby Shorthair

with rich black markings, black paw pads, and preferably a brick red nose, although black is allowed. Unlike most British Shorthairs they should have green or hazel eyes.

The Spotted Shorthair, once known as the Spotted Tabby, is related to the mackerel tabby. It has tabby face markings, but the stripes on the body have broken down into clearly defined spots. Only on the tail may the spots look like broken rings. It may be any of the colors recognized for tabbies with appropriately colored eyes.

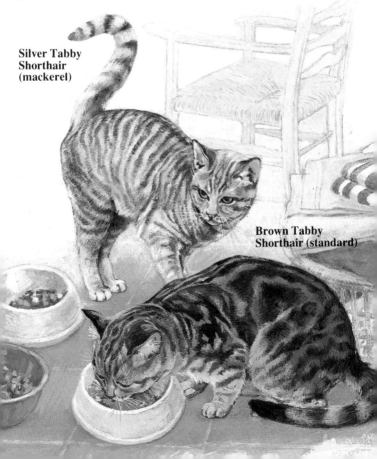

Silver Tabby Shorthair (mackerel)

Brown Tabby Shorthair (standard)

American Shorthairs

This breed, developed from cats taken to North America from Europe, is very like the British Shorthair. It has a medium to long body set on medium-length legs, giving it a rather longer look overall. The paws are round with heavy pads. The tail is medium long, heavy at the base and tapering to a blunt tip. The head, set on a slightly longer neck than that of the British cat, is less round, a little more heart-shaped and slightly deeper than it is wide. The ears are set well apart, but are less open at the base. The eyes are round and large with a slight hint of a slope at the outer upper edge. The coat is short and thick, and is recognized in a wider range of colors.

It may be White, with blue, orange, or odd eyes, and pink nose and paw pads; Black with golden eyes, black nose, and black or brown paw pads; Blue, in which a pale coat is preferred, with gold eyes, blue nose and paw pads; Cream, Bi-colored, Smoke, or

Red American Shorthair

26

Tortoiseshell. It is also recognized in Red, Chinchilla (equivalent to the British Tipped in black), and a darker version called the Shaded Silver. Shell Cameo and Shaded Cameo are the red equivalents of the last two and Smoke Cameo is a red version of Smoke (also

Smoke American Shorthair

Chinchilla American Shorthair

Shaded Silver American Shorthair

Shaded Cameo American Shorthair

known as Red Smoke). Tabbies may be all the colors of the European Tabby in either mackerel or standard pattern. Blue, Cream, and Cameo Tabby are also recognized. For the Tortoiseshell and White, American associations differ in their requirements for the white area of the coat. Some substitute a breed called the Calico, which has patches on a basically white coat and does not include cream in the patching. There is also a Dilute Calico with a white coat patched with areas of blue and cream. The Blue Cream requires the colors to be in separate patches, the exact opposite to the British Standard.

Tabby American Shorthairs

Cream

Silver

Blue

American Wirehair

Exotic Shorthair

Bombay

American breeders have also developed two short-haired cats with totally different coats. The American Wirehair is like the Shorthair except that its fur is medium long and wiry. It may be any color or pattern recognized in other breeds. The Exotic Shorthair is the result of crossing long-haired cats and American

Shorthairs. It has the physique and hair texture of the longhair or Persian cat but short fur, making it more like the British type than the American Shorthair. It may be any of the American Shorthair colors and patterns.

The Bombay is a black cat of Shorthair type, but with the sleek coat of the Burmese. It was developed by crossing these two breeds.

Manx Cats

The Manx gets it name from a small island in the Irish Sea, but that is not the only place where tailless cats have appeared. Unfortunately, taillessness is often linked with physical and health problems. To control risks Manx are not bred to Manx, but are crossed back to tailed cats.

Manx are short bodied with a rounded rump. In the true Manx the vertebrae that would form the base of the tail are completely missing and a hollow can be felt at the end of the spine. The rear legs are longer than the short front legs, making the back slope upward, even though the cat tends to bend the rear ones. This gives it a bouncy look, rather like a rabbit, when the cat is moving. The head should be like that of the American Shorthair with a dip in the nose or like that of the British Shorthair with a straight nose, prominent cheeks and pointed ears, set high upon the head. The fur is thick underneath with a longer outer coat, and may be any color or pattern recognized for other shorthairs.

Not all Manx are completely tailless, even if they were never bred out to tailed cats some would still carry the gene for a tail. In the U.S. some associations recognize as many as five different stages of Manx: Rumpy (tailless), Riser (with some vertebrae which can be seen or felt), Stumpy (with a moveable short tail), Longy (with a longer but reduced tail), and Tailed.

Stumpy (short-tailed) and Tailed Manx are now recognized in Britain. The tailed variety still looks distinctly different from the ordinary shorthair.

Manx cats

Rumpy

Stumpy

Longy

Other Shorthairs

The Cornish and Devon Rex cats both appeared as kittens of ordinary domestic cats in Britain. Their fur differs from that of other cats. It is a plush wavy coat with very noticeable crinkly hairs. Even the whiskers and eyebrows are crinkly. Earlier cats with curly hair had appeared in Germany. Such features have also cropped up in the U.S., where all Rex are grouped together. In Britain, Cornish and Devon are treated as distinct breeds. They are genetically different and if bred together produce only plain-coated kittens (although the next generation will include Rex). The Cornish has a body and head shape more like those of a Siamese cat and oval eyes, but round-tipped ears.

The Devon Rex has full cheeks, a short muzzle with a strong chin, a distinct break on the nose, and prominent whisker pads. Its ears are very large and set low on the head. The coat may be any color except bi-colored. Large, oval, sloping eyes match the coat except in the Si-Rex (marked like the Siamese) which

Scottish Fold

Devon Rex

Cornish Rex

must have chartreuse, green, or yellow eyes.

The Sphynx is a very rare variety. It has even less hair than the Rex, being covered only with a soft down, except for some wiry hair along the spine.

The Scottish Fold looks like an ordinary shorthair when a small kitten. Later its ears fold down like those of many dogs, a characteristic generally believed only to occur after many centuries of domestication.

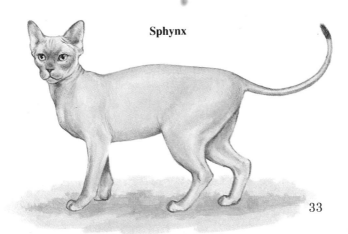

Sphynx

33

Foreign Shorthairs

This group has sleek coats and slim elegant bodies with long legs and tails which taper to a point. Their heads are wedge-shaped with large pricked ears and slanting, almond-shaped eyes. They tend to demand company and attention. They are also known as Oriental cats. Some did reach Europe from the East, but the name refers to the type and not to their place of origin.

The Russian Blue

This member of the group was the first to be known in Europe. At one time it was called the Archangel cat. It may be the same type as cats taken home from Russia by English sailors in Elizabeth I's time. The modern breed has a short, wedge-shaped head with straight nose, strong chin, and prominent whisker pads. Its large, pointed ears have little fur inside and such thin skin that you can see the light through them. Its eyes are a vivid green. The nose and paw pads are blue. The thick double coat is an even blue throughout and has a silky sheen.

Russian Blue

Siamese

Siamese cats were probably never common in Thailand, although they were known at the Thai court 400 years ago. Probably they originally came from further east. Some were taken from Bangkok to England in 1884, but there are reports of Siamese at a show a few years earlier. The restriction of the dark color of the coat to the "points" — head and ears, legs and tail — had been observed in cats long before. The overall color of the Siamese is always pale, whatever the points color, although the back may be a darker shade. Most Siamese kittens become gradually

Red Point Siamese

Blue Point Siamese

Lilac Point Siamese

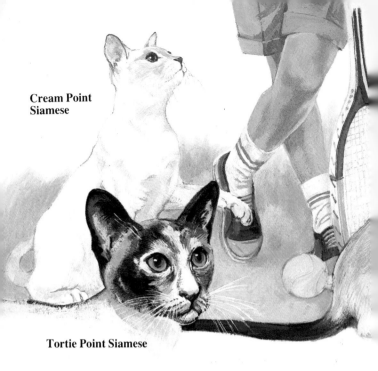

Cream Point Siamese

Tortie Point Siamese

darker as they get older. Kittens are born with a fluffy coat and no dark points. A patch around the nose appears first and reveals the color of future markings.

Siamese in early cat shows were much heavier in build and had a rounder head. Modern breeds have a smooth wedge-shaped head that narrows in straight lines from big, wide-based ears to a fine muzzle and strong chin. There must be neither pinching nor roundness in the cheeks, but a slight change of angle is allowable at the top of the nose. The almond-shaped eyes must be a clear deep blue except in lilac cats, when they may be paler.

The Seal Point was the first variety of Siamese to be recognized. It has a cream coat with rich, dark brown points. Blue Point, Chocolate Point, Lilac Point (with pinkish-grey points), Red Point, Tortie

Chocolate Point Siamese

Tabby Point Siamese

Seal Point Siamese

Point (Tortoiseshell), Blue Tortie (blue and cream), Chocolate Tortie (chocolate and red), and Lilac Tortie (lilac and pale cream) Points, Cream Point, and Tabby Point are now all recognized varieties.

In the U.S. some organizations recognize only the first four as Siamese and call the others Colorpoint Shorthairs. The Lilac used to be known as the Frost Point in the U.S. Tabby Points (which are known as Lynx Points in the U.S., Australia, and New Zealand) may be in any of the recognized Siamese colors. In the U.S. the paw pads of the Seal and Blue may also be pink. Those of the Chocolate are described as having a cinnamon pink nose and pink pads. In Europe the nose and paw pads should match the points color except in the Tabby Point, when they may also be pink.

Relations of the Siamese

In addition to the varieties of Siamese known as Colorpoint Shorthairs in the U.S., there is a group of cats belonging to the Siamese family in which the color is not restricted to the points and the coat is a solid color. In Europe these are the Foreign White, which has a pink nose and paw pads, and blue eyes; the Foreign Black which has black nose and pads with green eyes; and the Foreign Lilac, with pinkish nose and pads, and vivid green eyes.

In North America similar cats are known as Oriental Shorthairs. In addition to the White, Ebony (Black), and Lavender (Lilac) of Europe they may

Foreign Black

Foreign White

Foreign Lilac

also be Blue, Chestnut, Red, Cream, Silver, Cameo, Ebony Smoke, Blue Smoke, Chestnut Smoke, Lavender Smoke, Cameo Smoke, and various colors of Tabby. The White may have blue or green eyes; others should be green or amber.

The Havana is the solid-color similar to the Chocolate Siamese, except that it has green eyes and its coat is a darker chestnut brown. The whiskers and nose are chestnut and the paw pads are pinkish brown. The U.S. equivalent is the Havana Brown. It was developed from the British Havana. Breeding the Havana with non-Siamese has led to a heavier cat with a more rounded muzzle, round-tipped ears, and a sharper break in the profile. Its eyes are dark green and its nose rose.

Blue Oriental Shorthair

Havana

Cream Oriental Shorthair

Burmese

The Burmese, originally developed from a Siamese cross, looks distinctly different from a Siamese cat. It is heavy and muscular with a strong, rounded chest. The tail is of only medium length, tapers only slightly, and has a rounded tip. The head is more rounded on top, with full cheeks, tapering in a short, blunt wedge with a distinct break in the profile to a strong lower jaw. The ears tilt forward and have rounded tips. In the U.S. an even less Siamese look is required with

Chocolate Burmese

Blue Cream Burmese

Blue Burmese

Red Burmese

round eyes and round feet. The short, fine coat has a satiny texture and a glossy shine. It should be an even color shading to a lighter tone on the chest, belly, and inside of the legs; the face and ears may be a shade darker. The eyes may be any shade from amber to chartreuse, but a golden yellow is preferred.

The Brown Burmese has seal brown fur with nose and paw pads to match. In the U.S. it is known as the Sable Burmese. In Britain the Blue is a soft silver grey, but in the U.S. it is rich blue with pinkish blue-grey nose and pads. The Platignum, known only in the U.S., has pale silver-grey fur with fawn undertones and lavender-pink nose and pads.

Champagne, another American variety, has honey-beige fur with a brown nose and pinkish pads. In addition to these four colors, Britain recognizes five more. These are Chocolate (with pink nose and pads),

Burmese are friendly and intelligent cats. They are not as vocal or demanding as the Siamese.

Lilac Burmese

Brown Burmese

41

Tortie Burmese

Cream Burmese

Lilac, Red (a light tangerine with some tabby markings permitted on the face), Blue Cream (with the colors intermingled and nose and pads either plain or blotched blue and pink), Tortie, and Cream (with pink nose and pads).

Abyssinians

It has been claimed that this breed is directly descended from the cats of the Pharaohs. It was brought from Egypt by soldiers returning to Britain in the middle of the last century. The coat has similarities with that of the African Wildcat and with some cats in Egyptian paintings. Each hair is striped with two or three bands of darker color, a mutation of the tabby pattern. The Abyssinian is sleek and muscular. Its body is medium long with a fairly long, tapering tail and slim legs with small oval feet. The wedge-shaped head is broad and gently rounded. The muzzle is rounded with a slight indentation on each side. There is a firm chin and a slight rise from the top of the nose to the forehead. Ears are large, wide at the base, and pointed at the tip with tufts of hair. The large, almond-shaped eyes may be amber, hazel, or green in Europe. In the U.S. they are described as greenish-gold or hazel.

The original color, the Usual or Ruddy Abyssinian, is rich golden brown ticked with black. It has rich orange base hair. The tip of the tail and back of the hind legs are black, as are the paw pads. The nose is brick red. The Sorrel or Red Abyssinian has a lustrous copper-red body color flecked with chocolate, and deep apricot base hair. Nose and paw pads are pink. A Blue Abyssinian has blue-grey fur ticked with deeper steel blue. All colors have a line of dark color around the eyes and dark lines from the corner of the eyes up over the forehead. These may be set against lighter fur.

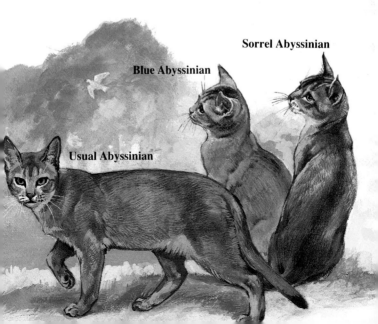

Sorrel Abyssinian

Blue Abyssinian

Usual Abyssinian

Other Foreign Shorthairs

The Korat, or Si-Sawat, which means "good fortune" in its native Thailand, is sturdy and muscular. It has a medium-long body and tail, and shorter legs than the Siamese. Heavy at the base, the tail tapers to a rounded tip. The heart-shaped face has a large flat forehead and the ears are large and upright with rounded tips. The silvery-blue coat is described in an ancient Thai poem as "smooth with roots like cloud and tips like silver."

The Egyptian Mau, or Oriental Spotted Tabby, is a conscious attempt to reproduce the cats in ancient Egyptian frescoes. It is like a spotted Siamese and known in Silver, Bronze, Smoke, and Pewter, each with brick red nose and dark paw pads, and Smoke, which has black nose and paw pads. All their eyes are bright green.

The Tonkinese, created by crossing an American Sable Burmese with a Siamese, is very Siamese looking. Its dark points still show, though they blend into the paler coat. Its feet are oval and its tail tapers. A warm brown coat with dark points is known as Natural Mink. A more reddish coat with reddish

Korat

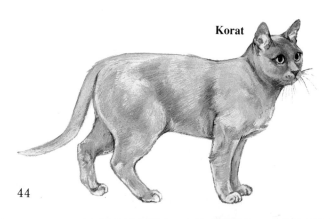

points is known as Honey Mink. Chocolate, Champagne, and Blue are also known.

The Japanese Bobtail, a native Japanese breed, is not so "foreign" in type as the previous cats. Its hind legs are longer than the front ones, but its most distinctive feature is a short tail. It is often curled back to make it look even shorter. The cat is accepted in many colors.

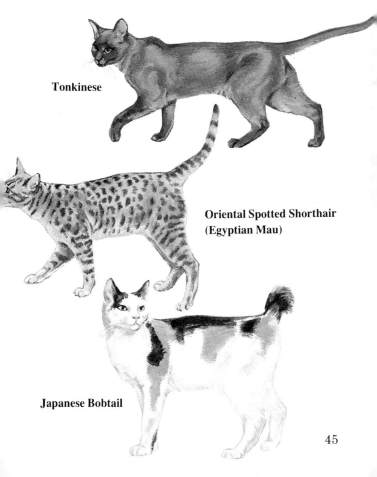

Tonkinese

Oriental Spotted Shorthair (Egyptian Mau)

Japanese Bobtail

45

Long-haired Cats

There is no record of long-haired cats in Europe until the sixteenth century, when travelers brought them back as curiosities from Turkey and Persia. The Turkish type, which we know today as the Angora, had a wedge-shaped head. The Persian has a more massive body and a rounder head. In the nineteenth century the Persian became the popular long-haired cat and has developed into today's show breed.

Longhairs have lush fur which it is not easy for the cat to keep in good condition. Daily brushing is necessary to prevent the cat from swallowing large quantities of fur which may cause blockage if not regurgitated as fur balls.

In the U.S. the breed is known as Persian. In Britain the breed is simply known as the Longhair. Its short, low lying body is carried on short, thick legs with large round feet. Its full tail does not taper. Its

White Longhair

head is round and broad with full cheeks and a short nose. In the U.S. the standard requires a definite break in the profile at the top of the nose. Its small ears are set low on the head and well apart. They tilt slightly forward and have rounded tips. The large, round eyes are usually copper or deep orange. The fur is extra long on the neck and chest, forming a ruff. There are tufts on the ears and between the toes.

The White Longhair can be blue, orange, or odd-eyed. Nose and paw pads are pink. As in Shorthairs, blue-eyed Whites are likely to be deaf. Black long-hairs should be pure black with black nose and paw pads. Blue Longhairs may be any shade of blue, provided the color is even, but in the U.S. a light blue is perferred. Nose and paw pads are blue.

Black Longhair

Blue Longhair

Red Longhairs have brick red nose and paw pads. Most red cats are male so Black and Tortoiseshell females are often mated with them to produce red kittens. Cream Longhairs have pink noses and paw pads. They are a pale shade of red and tend to be male. Chocolate and Lilac Longhairs have also been temporarily recognized.

American associations recognize a variation of the Red with a very short, slightly upturned nose and heavy wrinkles on the muzzle like a Pekinese dog. It is known as the Peke-faced Persian. Like Pug and Pekinese dogs, the flattening of the face can sometimes lead to breathing difficulties. Sometimes the folds of skin below the eyes may cause blocked tear ducts.

Smoke and Blue Smoke Longhairs have color tips on their top fur with a white undercoat. Their ruffs and ear tufts look silvery. Nose and paw pads match the tipping, which gives the effect of a solid color when the cat is not moving. In Britain a Pewter Longhair with white fur evenly shaded with black has

Cream Longhair

Red Longhair

Shaded Silver Persian

Chinchilla Longhair   **Peke-faced Persian**

been provisionally recognized. The Chinchilla has black tipping on the topcoat on the back, flanks, tail, head, and ears. Its emerald or blue-green eyes are heavily outlined in black. Its nose is brick red and its paw pads are black. Kittens are usually born with very dark fur. In the U.S. there is also a Shaded Silver Persian which has heavier tipping. Otherwise it is similar to the Chinchilla.

Smoke Longhair

Blue Smoke Longhair

49

Blue and White

Red and White

Bi-colored Longhairs

In Britain Bi-colored Longhairs may be any of the colors recognized for self-colored cats patched with white in clearly defined areas. These cats cannot be more than two-thirds colored nor more than half white, and with the face patched with both colors. In the U.S. only black, blue, red, or cream may be patched with white in the Parti-colored Persian. Nose and paw pads should match the coat color. A white blaze on the nose and forehead or an inverted "V" over the face is especially favored by breeders.

Cameo cats are the red equivalent of the Smoke and the Chinchilla, originally created by crossing Chinchilla and solid Red Longhairs. In the U.S. the undercoat is expected to be an ivory white. But in Britain it is described as "as white as possible." The Shell Cameo is palest, with the upper coat only very lightly tipped with red. This red gives it a pink blush over the top of the head, ears, back, and upper side of the tail. The rest of the cat, including the ear tufts, should be untipped. Nose and paw pads are rose and the eyes are outlined by rose-colored rims. The Shaded Cameo has slightly darker tipping and the Tortie Cameo has black, red, and cream tipping. The Smoke Cameo, or Red Smoke, is the red equivalent of the Smoke and Blue Smoke. It has an upper coat so heavily tipped that the cat looks red when not moving. Eye rims, nose, and paw pads are rose. In Britain Cream Cameos with cream instead of red tipping in Shell, Shaded, Cream Smoke, and Blue Cream are also provisionally recognized.

Smoke Cameo Persian

Shaded Cameo Persian

Shell Cameo Persian

Tortoiseshell Longhair

Tortoiseshell and White Longhair

Tortoiseshell Longhairs have patches of red, cream, and black evenly distributed over the coat, and a cream or red blaze on the face. Nose and paw pads should be color patched like the fur. Because tortoiseshells are female they are mated to Blacks, Creams, or Reds (if there is no sign of tabby

Blue Cream Longhair

Blue Cream Persian

markings), but there is no certainty that there will be any torties in a litter. In the British Tortoiseshell and White Longhair the white should intersperse the tortie color patching. Some American standards ask for white legs and the upper parts tortie with white splashed on the nose and around the neck.

The Calico Persian is an American variety which is like the Tortoiseshell but with red, cream, and black patching on a white ground. Its belly is white with predominantly white areas on the chest, legs, and paws. Its face has a white blaze. In the Dilute Calico Persian the color patching is in blue and cream.

Blue Cream Longhairs have the colors intermingled in the British cat. The colors are distinctly separated in the American variety. American breeders like to see a cream blaze on the face.

Sometimes the Calico cat replaces the Tortoiseshell and White as a breed; in other U.S. associations both are recognized.

Calico Persian

Dilute Calico Persian

Tabby Longhairs

Tabby Longhairs may be either mackerel or standard in pattern provided that the pattern is clearly defined. British cats can be Brown, Red, or Silver; American Tabby Persians can be these colors and Blue, Cream, and Cameo Tabby as well. The British standard for the Tabby Longhair does not specifically mention the oyster blotch described in the Shorthair standard. Otherwise the requirements for the two patterns are identical.

The Brown has clear black markings on brown with a red nose and black or brown paw pads. Its eyes are copper or hazel. The Red has dark red markings on light red with a brick red nose and pink paw pads. Its eyes are deep copper. The Silver has black markings

Cameo Tabby Persian

Red Tabby Longhair

54

Blue Tabby Persian

on a silver ground with a red nose and black paw pads. Its eyes are bright green or hazel, not the orange of most longhairs. Sometimes the Silver tends to have a less flattened head than other longhairs. It can be an extremely beautiful cat.

The Cream Tabby Persian has buff or dark cream markings on a paler cream ground with pink nose and paw pads. The lips and chin should be pale cream. Its eyes are bright copper or gold. The Blue Tabby Persian's coat is a pale bluish-ivory ground color, including lips and chin, with deep blue markings. Its nose and paw pads are rose and its eyes copper or gold. The Cameo Tabby Persian has an off-white ground color with red markings. Its nose and paw pads are rose. Its eyes are bright copper or gold.

Brown Tabby Longhair

Cream Tabby Persian

Silver Tabby Longhair

Other Long-haired Cats

The Maine Coon Cat is probably the result of matings between the original short-haired cats taken to North America from Europe and Angora cats introduced by later travelers. They probably ran wild in Maine and other New England states.

They are sturdily built and often large in size. Sometimes they can look dainty with their high cheekbones, upright pointed ears, long nose, and oval eyes. Body, tail, and neck are long. The rugged coat, which protected them through the tough winters of New England, is short on the shoulders, lengthening toward the tail and forming heavy "breeches." A full ruff begins below the tufted ears, meeting across the chest. The fur may be white, black, cream, tortoiseshell, tortoiseshell and white, calico, blue-cream, bi-color, any type of tabby, or tabby and white. Nose and paw pads should match the coat. Eyes may be of any color.

Maine Coon Cat

Colorpoints, known as Himalayan cats in the U.S., are of the usual longhair or Persian type with long fur, but with the Siamese points pattern. They are recognized in Seal, Chocolate, Lilac, Red, Tortie, Cream, Blue Cream, Chocolate Cream, and Lilac Cream in Britain. In the U.S. they can also be Red, Lilac, Chocolate, or Seal Lynx Point, or variations of the Tortie Point with red and/or cream ground color combined with seal, cream, blue, or lilac. The British Colorpoint must not be confused with the American Colorpoint Shorthair—they are totally different in shape and coat.

The Birman, at first glance, looks like the Colorpoint. A closer look will reveal a longer nose, longer legs and tail, and larger ears. The fur is long and silky, tending to curl on the belly. The tail is plumelike. The Birman is said to have definite links with the East. When first taken to France the Birman was known as the Sacred Cat of Burma. Legends tell of it guarding temples in the country. In Europe the coat is

Chocolate Colorpoint

Red Colorpoint

Blue Point Birman

described as golden beige. Its nose and paw pads are pink. The Blue Point has a bluish-white body color shading to white on the stomach, with deep blue points. Its nose is slate grey and paw pads pink. In the U.S., Chocolate and Lilac varieties are also recognized. All have blue eyes. Their coat patterns differ from the Colorpoint and the Siamese; they have white paws and on the hind legs the white extends up

Cymric

the back of the leg to end in a point. These white paws make the breed immediately distinguishable.

The Cymric is another cat that could not be mistaken for any other breed. Its name means "Welsh" in the Welsh language. It is a long-haired version of the Manx. In the U.S. it is known as the Manx Longhair. The medium-length coat is softer than that of the normal Manx. It is not yet recognized in Britain.

The Somali is a long-haired version of the Abyssinians cat with the same body shape, but the banded fur is long and silky in this breed. It has a full ruff, plumelike tail, and plenty of fur on the hind legs. There are tufts of hair both inside and on the tips of its ears. It may be either Red or Ruddy.

The Balinese is another cat recognized in the U.S. and is being bred in Britain. It is a long-haired version of the Siamese and has all the physical features of the Siamese except for the length of the coat. It also retains the character of the Siamese cat.

Red Somali

Ruddy Somali

The Angora was probably the first type of long-haired cat to be known in Europe. It came from Turkey and was named after the Turkish capital city we now know as Ankara. Its long silky fur is like mohair, the fur of the Angora goat which comes from the same part of the world. It has a longish body and tail and a small, neat head with large almond-shaped eyes that slope slightly, and large pointed ears. The face is longer, narrower, and more pointed than the Persian and with a slightly longer nose. The legs are long with small, dainty paws. The fur lies close to the back and sides of the body and the head. Longer fur hangs from the body and forms a full ruff and breeches, with long tufts in the ears and a flowing tail.

The Angora had almost disappeared by the beginning of this century, but was revived by a special breeding program at Ankara Zoo. Four cats taken to the U.S. in the 1960s re-established the breed in the West. Angoras are bred, but not yet re-established as a breed in Britain.

Balinese

The Turkish cat, or Turkish Van, is a naturally occurring type from the area around Lake Van, high in the mountains of eastern Turkey. There is snow for six months of the year in their native territory. The cats are hardy animals, males being particularly muscular. This breed is closer in type to the Angora than to any other cat, with a long, sturdy body, and medium-length legs on rounded feet. They have long, silver-white fur with auburn markings on the face, extending from the base of the white ears and leaving a white blaze on the forehead. The tail is auburn with slightly darker rings. Nose, paw pads, and the inside of the ears are a delicate pink. The eyes are round and light amber.

Turkish

Angora

Index